Traditions Around the World

by Anita Ganeri

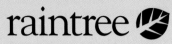

a Capstone company — publishers for children

Engage Literacy is published in the UK by Raintree.
Raintree is an imprint of Capstone Global Library Limited, a company incorporated in England and Wales
having its registered office at 264 Banbury Road, Oxford, OX2 7DY – Registered company number:
6695582

www.raintree.co.uk

Editorial credits
Marissa Kirkman and Jennifer Huston, editors; Peggie Carley, Lisa King and Charmaine Whitman, designers;
Morgan Walters, media researcher; Katy LaVigne, production specialist

Image credits
Alamy: Science History Images, 18; iStockphoto: SilviaJansen, 14, 30; Shutterstock: Aleksandar Todorovic, 6,
Alizada Studios, 28, AmyLv, 11, artjazz, bottom 16, Byelikova Oksana, top 23, middle 23, chasdesign,
bottom right Cover, Click Bestsellers, design element throughout, Cover, Clive Chilvers, top 16, Deborah Kolb,
9, Elena11, top 8, elina, 15, Evgeny Bendin, 31, GRSI, bottom 24, Iurii Osadchi, 19, JASPERIMAGE, bottom
8, top 24, Jefferson Bernardes, 20, Kobby Dagan, 17, Kucher Serhii, back cover, Kzenon, top left Cover,
magicinfoto, 4, MaraZe, 12, marco mayer, top 13, margouillat photo, bottom 13, miya227, middle Cover,
1, oksana.perkins, left 21, Peter Hermes Furian, top 7, Rainer Lesniewski, bottom 23, Rawpixel.com, bottom
5, 25, Rolf_52, 26, T photography, 22, TeodorLazarev, bottom 7, theskaman306, 29, Uncle-Duck, 10,
wavebreakmedia, bottom left Cover, top 5, windmoon, 27, XiXinXing, top right Cover; Thinkstock:
StephenChing, right 21

Traditions Around the World

ISBN: 978-1-4747-4699-1

Printed and bound in India

Contents

Around the world 4

Clothing 6

Food. 10

Going to school. 14

Music and dance. 16

Playing sport 18

Happy holidays!. 22

Everyday life 28

Glossary 31

Index 32

Around the world

What sort of food do you like to eat? Where do you go to school? How do you celebrate special days? Do you play any sports? People live their lives in different ways in many countries around the world. The ways people do things and the ideas they share that are passed down over time are called *traditions*. Some traditions might be just like yours. Others might seem very different. Are you ready to explore?

Clothing

The type of clothes people wear can be a tradition. Some groups of people choose clothing based on the weather where they live. In other places, clothes are made with the items that people have found nearby. Over time, groups of people pass down a type of clothing to their children. As they grow, the children may wear these clothes to celebrate special days.

In the countries of Kenya and Tanzania, in Africa, it is warm in the day and cool at night. The Maasai people who live there wear long, loose clothes called *shukas*. Red is a popular colour for shukas because it means that the one who wears it is brave.

The Maasai people wear brightly coloured shukas.

The Arctic is an area all around the North Pole.

The Inuit people live in the Arctic, where it is freezing cold all year. Long ago, Inuit people learned that wearing animal skins and furs kept them warm. Many people in this part of the world still wear clothes and boots made from animal skins and furs.

Inuit people live where it is very cold.

kimono

In some countries, it is a tradition for people to dress up in special clothes for events such as festivals. A *kimono* is a silk dress from Japan. It has long sleeves and a wide belt. Today kimonos are mostly worn at festivals, weddings and other special events.

During special events in Scotland, men and boys sometimes wear *kilts*. Kilts are pleated skirts made from woollen cloth with a special pattern. Hundreds of years ago, soldiers wore them when they went into battle.

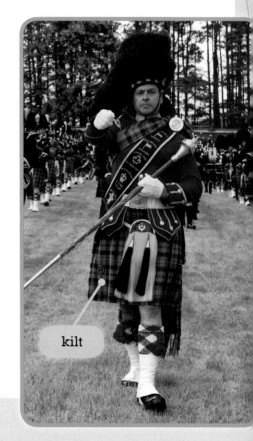
kilt

sari

A *sari* is a very long piece of cloth. Saris have been worn by women in India for more than 5,000 years. Many women still wear them every day. A sari is wrapped around the waist and over one shoulder. Many parts of India have their own special sari designs. Certain colours and patterns are worn for different seasons and festivals.

Food

Food holds special meaning to people around the world. Because of this, eating certain foods has become a tradition in many parts of the world.

People have been eating noodles in China for thousands of years. They believe that noodles represent long life and good health. The noodles are served in a bowl and eaten with *chopsticks* instead of a knife and fork. Chinese people believe that chopsticks can bring good luck.

In China, noodles are eaten with chopsticks.

Pasta comes in many different shapes.

Italy has a long tradition of eating noodles called pasta. Pasta comes in many sizes and shapes. Pasta is made from wheat mixed with water or eggs. A special type of wheat grows in Italy that allows pasta dough to dry and harden. This dried pasta is able to sit on a shelf to be boiled and eaten later. Today, people in many countries around the world enjoy eating pasta.

Before there were refrigerators, it was hard to preserve food, or keep it fresh, for long periods of time. Long ago in Japan, people learned that rice could be used to keep fish fresh for longer. People would salt the raw fish and then wrap it in cooked rice. This kept the fish fresh for months at a time. In the past, *sushi*, or raw fish with rice, was mostly eaten by the rich. Today sushi is no longer just for the rich. Many people in Japan and other countries eat sushi.

sushi

Tagine is a North African dish made from meat, fish or vegetables. It is cooked very slowly over a fire in a big clay pot. Tagine was most likely first

tagine

cooked hundreds of years ago. Today people add dried fruit, peppers or nuts to give the dish a sweet or spicy taste.

FACT: A hot dog is a type of sausage served in a bun. It is an American tradition to serve hot dogs at summer barbecues and baseball games.

Going to school

Children learn about traditions at school, and they take part in them, too. When children in Germany start school, they are given a special gift called a school cone. This large paper cone is filled with toys, sweets, pencils and books. Receiving a

This girl is carrying her school cone.

school cone has been a tradition for children in Germany since 1810.

In the United States many children begin every school day by saying the Pledge of Allegiance. This is a promise to be loyal to their country. They make this promise standing in front of the American flag with their hands on their hearts. American children have been following this tradition since 1892.

This girl is ringing the bell for Knowledge Day.

In Russia the school year begins on 1 September. Since 1984 this has been called Knowledge Day. Children dress up in their best clothes and arrive carrying bunches of flowers. The flowers are given to the teachers. One of the youngest children rings the first bell to start the new school year.

Music and dance

steel drum

Countries around the world have their own music and dance traditions. *Calypso* is a catchy style of music from Trinidad. It is based on the music that people from Africa brought with them when they were taken to Trinidad to work. Calypso music is played on instruments made from steel oil drums.

Flamenco dance is a tradition that started in the south of Spain. Flamenco began with groups of people who lived in this part of Spain hundreds of years ago. Female flamenco dancers usually wear red, white or black dresses. They tap out the beat with their heels and hands. Male dancers wear black trousers, a white shirt and a vest or jacket.

flamenco dancer

Irish step dancers

Dancing has been a tradition in Ireland for thousands of years. Dance teachers in brightly coloured clothes would travel all over the country. They taught people the latest dance steps. One type of Irish dancing is called step dancing. The dancers keep their upper bodies still while their feet move very quickly. Female dancers wear brightly coloured dresses. They also have a cape hanging from their shoulders. Boys and men wear plain kilts and jackets. They also wear capes.

Playing sport

The sports that people play are often traditions for that country. Most sports began long ago as games and were passed down over time. Today's sport of lacrosse dates back to American Indians in the 1600s. They played this game with a crooked stick and a ball made of leather. Today lacrosse is played around the world.

American Indians playing lacrosse

ice hockey

Ice hockey is the national sport in Canada. There are a few ideas about how the sport of ice hockey began. Most agree that ice hockey is made up of parts of other sports. These include field hockey, lacrosse and an Irish game called *hurling*. Ice hockey has become a tradition in Canada. Many people from Canada play ice hockey on teams around the world.

FACT: For many years, people thought ice hockey was invented in Canada. But it seems that British soldiers and settlers may have brought the game to Canada in the 1800s. Players changed the rules of field hockey to be played on the ice.

The first football match in Brazil took place in 1894. Today football is Brazil's national sport. The team from Brazil is one of the best in the world. They have won the World Cup a record five times.

Brazil's star player, Neymar (left), tries to protect the ball during a World Cup match.

archer

target

The biggest sporting event in Bhutan is an *archery* contest. Around 260 teams take part, and the event lasts for three months. Hundreds of years ago, bows and arrows were used for hunting and war. Today archery is Bhutan's national sport and the top archers become famous. Archers shoot their arrows at a target to win an event.

Happy holidays!

Holidays are special days full of many traditions. Carnival is a yearly festival in Brazil. It has been held before the Easter holiday every year since 1723. Over time this festival has changed as ideas and traditions have been brought to Brazil from other countries. Today there's an exciting parade with dancers, music and floats. The dancers are dressed in brightly coloured costumes that take many months to make. Carnival is a favourite tradition in Brazil.

Brazil's Carnival parade

costumes for the Day of the Dead

Costumes are also part of the traditional Day of the Dead festival in Mexico. This holiday began with the Aztecs, who are people native to the land. The Day of the Dead begins at midnight on 1 November. During this festival, people think about loved ones who have died, but it is not a gloomy time. People take flowers to the graves of their loved ones. Children wear special costumes and are given gifts of sugar skulls as a treat.

sugar skulls

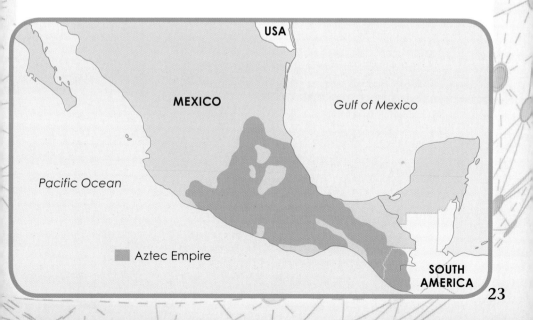

USA

MEXICO

Gulf of Mexico

Pacific Ocean

Aztec Empire

SOUTH AMERICA

23

Scotland's Highland Games are held in the summer. This festival is full of traditions. It includes sport, music and dancing. The most famous event is tossing the *caber*. For this event, a tree trunk (called a caber) is thrown into the air. There is also a Scottish dancing contest, and people play music on the *bagpipes*. Many people wear kilts to this festival.

tossing the caber

bagpipes

A family joins together at the table to celebrate Thanksgiving.

On the fourth Thursday in November, people in the United States celebrate Thanksgiving. The first Thanksgiving was held in 1621. *Colonists* who had moved to America from England joined together with American Indians for a meal to celebrate a good *harvest*. The tradition carries on today as many American families enjoy a special dinner of roast turkey and pumpkin pie.

In Sweden the start of the Christmas season is marked by St Lucia's Day. This day celebrates Saint Lucia, a girl who brought food to those in need. One girl is chosen as Lucia. She wears a red sash and a crown of candles on her head. She leads a parade of other girls dressed in long, white dresses and carrying candles.

St Lucia's Day

a Chinese New Year parade

All over the world, a new year is a time for a fresh start. Chinese New Year falls in January or February. People clean their homes and buy new clothes to mark this tradition. Dancers dress up as dragons and twist and turn their way through the city streets.

Everyday life

Traditions can also be found in the things people do every day. Even the way people say "hello" to each other can be a tradition.

In New Zealand people touch their foreheads and noses together at the same time to say "hello". This tradition is called a "hongi". It began with the Maori people, who were the first people to live in New Zealand. It is a sign of respect to share breath with each other.

These two men are greeting each other in New Zealand.

namaste

In other countries, such as India, people put their hands together and bow their heads slightly without touching each other. As they bow, they say "namaste", which means "I bow to you". This act shows respect for the other person. People use this sign of respect to say both "hello" and "goodbye" to others.

In Japan it is a tradition to take off your shoes before you go inside. There, the floors of some homes are covered

in straw mats. It is polite to take off your shoes and put on a pair of slippers instead. This tradition dates back to around the year 800. It is likely that this tradition began as a way to keep the floors clean. People at that time would sit, eat and sleep on mats on the floor.

Some traditions are just for fun. In Greece if two people say the same thing at the same time, they shout "touch red" and must touch something red. This is believed to stop them from getting into a fight.

These are only a few of the many traditions people follow around the world. What traditions do you follow?

Glossary

archery sport of shooting at targets using a bow and arrow

bagpipes musical instrument played especially in Scotland that consists of a bag for air, a mouth tube for blowing up the air bag and pipes that give a sound when air passes through them

caber young tree trunk tossed in a traditional Scottish sport

Calypso lively style of music from the West Indies

chopsticks two narrow sticks used to eat food; chopsticks are used mostly by people from Asian countries

colonist person who lives in a colony, a land ruled by another country

flamenco fast and lively Spanish dance

harvest crop gathered in a single season

hurling Irish game similar to field hockey played between two teams of 15 players each

kilt knee-length tartan skirt, often worn by Scottish men as part of their traditional costume

kimono long, loose robe with wide sleeves and a sash

sari long piece of cloth that is wrapped around a woman's body

shuka long, loose item of clothing worn by the Maasai people of Africa

sushi Japanese food made of raw fish or seafood pressed into rice

tagine stew from northwest Africa that is cooked in a clay pot

tradition custom, idea or belief passed down through time

Index

Africa 6, 16

American Indians 18, 25

Arctic 7

Aztec people 23

Bhutan 21

Brazil 20, 22

Canada 19

China 10

chopsticks 10

clothing 6–9

    kilt 8, 17, 24

    kimono 8

    sari 9

    shuka 6

dancing 16–17, 24

    flamenco 17

    Irish step dancing 17

England 19

food 10–13

    hot dog 13

    noodles 10, 11

    pasta 11

    sushi 12

    tagine 13

Germany 14

Greece 30

holidays 22–27

    Carnival 22

    Chinese New Year 27

    Christmas 26

    Day of the Dead 23

    Easter 22

    St Lucia's Day 26

    Thanksgiving 25

hongi 28

India 9, 29

Inuit people 7

Ireland 17, 19

Italy 11

Japan 8, 12, 30

Maasai people 6

Maori people 28

Mexico 23

music 16–17, 24

    bagpipes 24

    Calypso 16

namaste 29

New Zealand 28

North Pole 7

Russia 15

school 14–15

    Knowledge Day 15

    Pledge of Allegiance 14

Scotland 8, 24

Spain 16

sport 18–21

    archery 21

    baseball 13

    caber toss 24

    field hockey 19

    football 20

    Highland Games 24

    hurling 19

    ice hockey 19

    lacrosse 18, 19

    World Cup 20

Sweden 26

Trinidad 16

United States 13, 14, 25